dancing bears

BOOK A

by
Hilary & Tom Burkard

Stories illustrated by
Angie Lyndon.

Other original artwork by
Adam Jones & Hilary Burkard

First published 2001, The Promethean Trust
Second Edition (Revised) 2002, The Promethean Trust
Third Edition (Revised) 2004, Hilary Burkard
Fourth Edition (Revised) 2005, Hilary Burkard
Fifth Edition (Revised) 2006, Hilary Burkard

Tracing exercises produced using *Handwriting for Windows*
available from: www.kber.co.uk

Copyright © Hilary Burkard 2006

All rights reserved. No part of this publication may be reproduced or transmitted in any form or by any means, electronic or mechanical, including photocopying, recording, or any information storage or retrieval system, without the written permission of the authors.

ISBN: 1-905174-10-1
ISBN-13: 978-1-905174-10-2

PUBLISHED BY HILARY BURKARD
MMVI

DISTRIBUTED BY
SOUND FOUNDATIONS
RIVERSIDE FARM, EASTON, NORWICH. NR9 5EP.
www.soundfoundationsbooks.co.uk
sales@soundfoundationsbooks.co.uk
☎ 01603 881158 **FAX** 01603 882170

dancing bears

Contents:

Introduction:
- The Ground Rules 6
- The Teaching Techniques 7

Absolute beginners:
- Oral Blending with pictures 11

Tenderfoot Level:
- Transfer of oral blending to print 16

Level 1:
- Decoding Power Pages 28
- ee, ar, sh, I, the 30
- th, me, you, ... 32
- ck, he, she 36
- er, my, why 41
- Cloze sentences 43
- we, be 44
- said, by 46
- or, ch, qu, Qu, and, fly 49
- to, do, who 52
- try 53
- give, have, live 54
- ay, oy 57
- are, so, no, go 58
- Word sums, ai 61

Level 2
- oi, oa 69
- was 72
- Final Consonant Blends 78
- they 80
- air, oar, eer, ore, of 84
- some 86

Level 3
- Fluency Reading 93
- here 95
- where, there 98
- Initial Consonent Blends 111
- saw, come, put 116
- could, your 128
- should, would 133

3

dancing bears — Introduction:

- **dancing bears** is a complete decoding programme for slow readers. You won't need any other books.

- **No lesson-planning.** Just 10 minutes a day with each pupil.

- **dancing bears** works with all children, whatever their problems or learning styles. Try it, and you'll see.

- **dancing bears** is simple and straightforward. Teachers, assistants and parents can all use it successfully. No synthetic phonics classroom can afford to be without it.

- **Suitable for pupils of any age from 4+.**

The Ground Rules:

1. Whatever you do, don't force children to 'work it out for themselves'. When they can't read a word, just tell them what it is. **You don't want to make reading into a struggle.**

2. Don't give ticks for a 'good try'. Just practise it, and go back to it the next day.

3. Keep the lesson going at a cracking pace! Kids' minds work a lot faster than ours do.

4. Daily lessons are essential. If you can't find 10 minutes per day for each slow reader, there is something wrong with your priorities.

The Teaching Techniques:

1. **Using the flashcards**—oddly enough, this is the hardest part! If you didn't grow up playing bridge or poker, just handling the cards can be tricky. Be sure you read the instructions carefully.

2. **Using the cursor**—This is quite easy to learn. The cursor trains the child to read from left to right, and it trains them to look at every letter in a word.

3. **The 'Flashback' technique**—After you have corrected an error, you must return to the same item again.

All this is explained on the following pages. Please read them carefully.

Using the flashcards:

There are two sets of flashcards. The first one is printed on green card. You will use this set right at the beginning. The second set, printed on blue card, is not used until you finish Level 2.

Cut up the green flashcards along the lines printed on the back. It is important to cut them accurately—the cards are hard to handle if they are all different sizes.

All the flashcards are numbered. It is important to teach them in order—the lowest number first. First, you must find out which sounds your pupil already knows. Present the flashcards one at a time, and ask what sound the letter makes. If the child gives the letter name, say

"That's the *name* of the letter. But what *sound* does it make?"

If the pupil says the right sound, 'give' him the card by putting it in a pile in front of him. When you have finished going through the flashcards, this pile will go into the pocket inside the front cover of the book, and he will practice these every day. This will help him respond quickly and automatically.

Keep a separate pile for all the flashcards he doesn't know. These will go into the pocket inside the back cover. You will introduce these—starting with the lowest numbered card. Most pupils can learn a new sound every day. If your child is severely dyslexic, 2 or 3 a week is about right.

Introducing a new sound:

Go through the cards in the back pocket and pick out the one with the lowest number. This is your new sound for the day. Present this card to the pupil and say;

"This card makes the sound *xx*. What sound?"

Make sure he pronounces the sound correctly. If he has a speech defect, make sure that he pronounces it the same as he does in a word.

Then pick out three more flashcards that the pupil already knows well. Mix the new card in with them, and keep presenting them until the new sound is pronounced correctly every time. If the pupil is really having problems, just shuffle it back one place. That way, he doesn't have to remember it for very long.

The next day, the pupil may well have forgotten the new sound. If he does, just tell him what it is, get him to repeat it and then shuffle the card back one place. That way, he will get it right the second time, and it will not worry him. In a few days, he should get it right the first time he sees it.

Any time your pupil gets a sound wrong, just tell him what the sound is, and then shuffle the card back one place. **Never, never** make a big deal of it. The whole point of dancing bears is to make reading easy. If a pupil doesn't say the right answer straight away, you must tell him what it is—and then make him repeat it.

When do I stop using the green flashcards?

When the pupil can say the sounds quicker than you can flip the flashcards, you can stop using them. Usually, you will have to keep on using the digraphs (two-letter flashcards) for a bit longer.

Using the Cursor:

A cursor is a piece of card about the size of a business card, and it has a small notch cut out of one corner. You will use it to reveal letters (or digraphs) one at a time, so that the child gets used to scanning words from left to right. **You must use the cursor at all times.**

When children are taught to read whole words, their eyes often jump all over the place, trying to scramble the letters to make a 'fit' with a word they know.   With the cursor, children learn to read what is actually on the page.

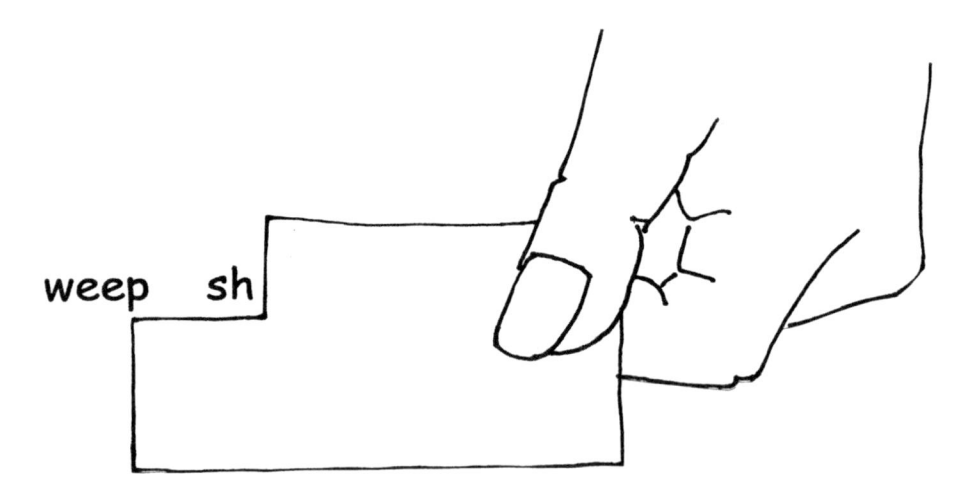

The Flashback Technique:

We use the **Flashback Technique** every time a pupil makes an error. If you go back to the instructions for using the flashcards, you will see that when a pupil does not make the correct response, you tell him what it is. Then you bury the flashcard one card back, so it comes up again while it is still fresh in his immediate memory. This is an example of the Flashback Technique.

We also use it when a pupil is reading words. Any time a pupil fails to read the word, correct him, get him to repeat it and go on to the next item. Then go back to the one he just missed. When you have finished a line, go back again to any words missed. When you have finished the exercise for the day, go back over all words missed again. This way, the pupil will usually earn his tick for the line the next day. (Remember—you never tick a line when the pupil gets it right on the second go—you must wait until the next day.)

dancing bears — Absolute Beginners:

All non-readers start here.

Pupils who can read simple three-letter words should start at page 28.

Oral Blending with pictures:
(NB: In addition to doing these exercises, you must be practising the green flashcards at least once a day)

Tell your pupil that you are going to say some words, but they will be broken up. All he has to do is to point to the right picture.

Look at page 12. You will start with the first three pictures in **Series 1**—the dog, the cat, and the man. Cover up the rest of the pictures on the page to avoid confusion. Tell your pupil that there is a cat, a dog and a man. Ask him to point to each in turn. Then tell him that the sounds /c/a/t/ make the word 'cat'. Ask him to point to the cat. Then say the sounds /d/o/g/—but this time, he has to put the word together and point to the right picture. If he doesn't get it, tell him the word.

Keep doing these three items in random order until the pupil gets it right every time. If your pupil is not getting tired or frustrated, go on and do the second and third rows of pictures in Series 1. If your pupil is catching on quickly, you can even mix items from all three lines. Remember that the pupil is blending the *sounds* in each word—which is not always the individual letters. In *bird*, the letters *i* and *r* make the sound /er/, not /i/r/. The pictures are labeled for the benefit of the teacher, at this stage the pupil is only learning to put sounds together to make words—reading the words comes later.

Oral Blending with pictures: Series 1

Remember to practise the flashcards at least once a day.

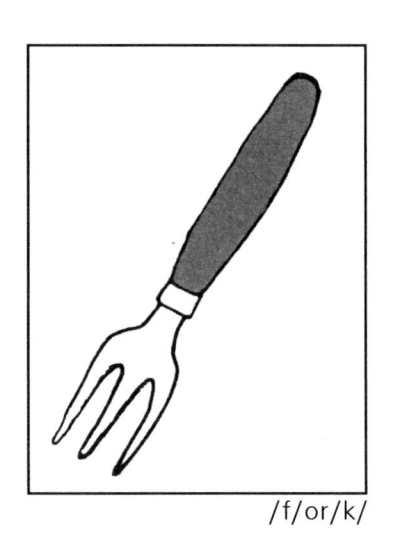

/c/a/t/	/d/o/g/	/m/a/n/
/b/ir/d/	/c/a/n/	/f/or/k/
/c/ar/	/l/o/ck/	/b/u/g/

Oral Blending with pictures: Series 2

Add a new flashcard every day.

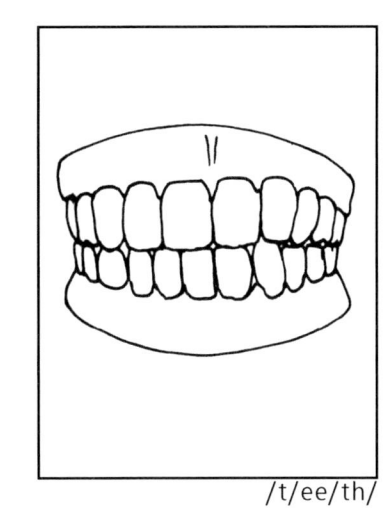

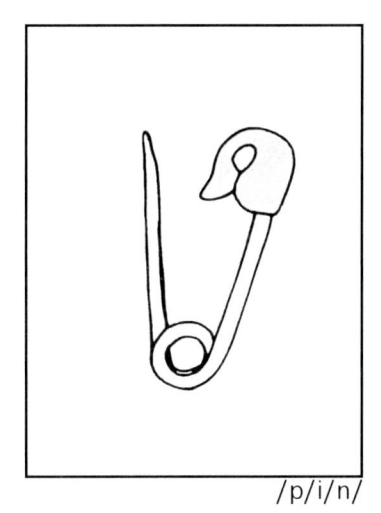

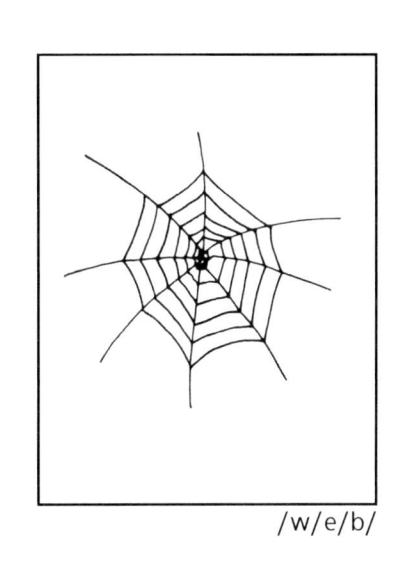

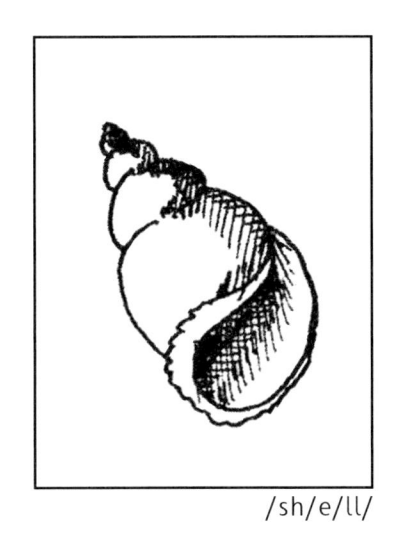

/d/u/ck/   /t/ee/th/   /p/i/n/

/t/oa/d/   /w/e/b/   /h/or/se/

/sh/e/ll/   /d/o/ll/   /sh/ee/p/

Oral Blending with pictures: Series 3

/j/a/m/   /p/i/g/   /z/i/p/

/s/o/ck/   /f/i/sh/   /b/a/t/

/j/u/g/   /c/ow/   /m/a/p/

Oral Blending with pictures: Series 4

Don't forget the flashcards!

/b/oo/k/	/sh/ar/k/	/sh/i/p/
/g/u/ll/	/g/oa/t/	/g/ir/l/
/c/u/p/	/c/a/p/	/c/o/p/

dancing bears   Tenderfoot Level:

Transfer of oral blending to print—how to use the 'Tenderfoot' pages:

First—
Pupils trace letters, saying sounds as they write them.

s a t p i n

Nothing to this—if necessary, guide the pupil's hand. *(Children who find handwriting difficult will benefit greatly from our* **apples and pears** *spelling and writing programme.)*

Second—
- You say the sounds in 'sat' as you move the cursor. Then you ask, "What word?"

Oral   trace   read
sat   sat   sat

☐☐☐☐   ☐☐☐☐   ☐☐☐☐

Third—

- The pupil traces the word, saying the sounds. Again, you ask "What word?"

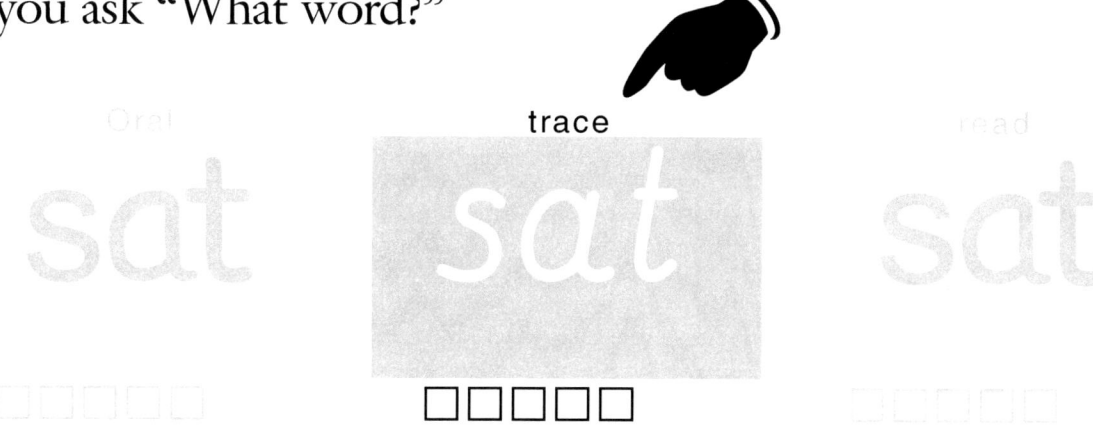

trace

sat

Fourth—

- You move the cursor and ask the pupil to say the sounds himself. Once more, you ask "What word?"

read

sat

This is virtually fool-proof—but it's still a big deal, the child has read his (or her) first word! Congratulations are in order! Repeat this procedure with the next two words on the page.

Fifth—

sat pin tap ☐

- Using the cursor, ask the pupil to say the sounds in each word, and then ask "What word?"

- If the pupil gets all three right, tick the box at the bottom. You are done with this page!

- If the pupil cannot read all of the words, repeat all of the above exercises the following day. Even the most 'dyslexic' pupils will catch on in a few days.

s a t p i n

Remember to practise the flashcards at least once a day.

Oral — trace — read

sat　sat　sat
☐☐☐☐　☐☐☐☐　☐☐☐☐

pin　pin　pin
☐☐☐☐　☐☐☐☐　☐☐☐☐

tap　tap　tap
☐☐☐☐　☐☐☐☐　☐☐☐☐

sat　pin　tap ☐

c o h p a n

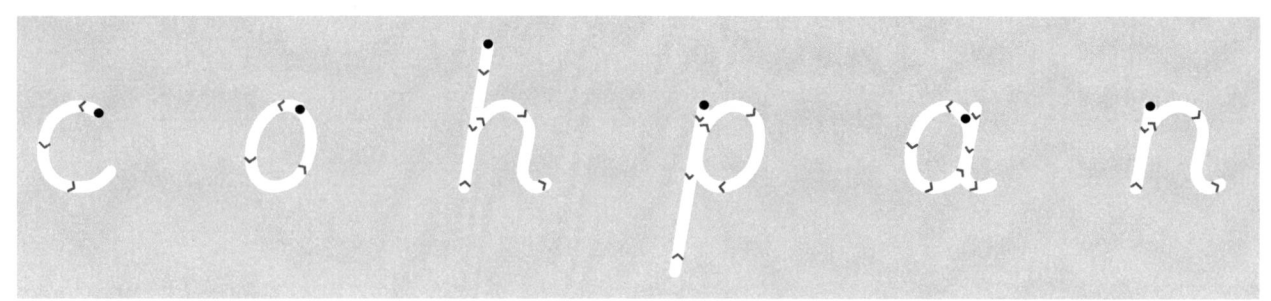

Do not award ticks for a 'good try'—your pupil will pay for it later!

Oral	trace	read
cat	cat	cat
☐☐☐☐	☐☐☐☐	☐☐☐☐
hot	hot	hot
☐☐☐☐	☐☐☐☐	☐☐☐☐
pan	pan	pan
☐☐☐☐	☐☐☐☐	☐☐☐☐

cat hot pan ☐

20

g r e p i t

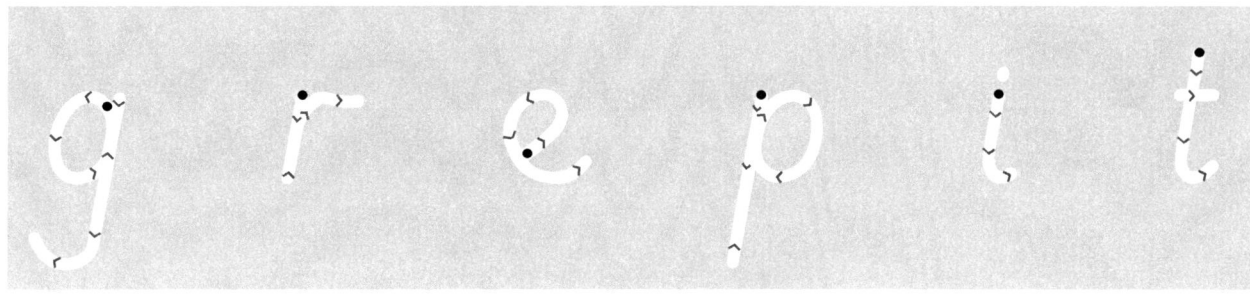

Always use the cursor!

Oral   trace   read

rat   rat   rat

☐☐☐☐   ☐☐☐☐   ☐☐☐☐

get   get   get

☐☐☐☐   ☐☐☐☐   ☐☐☐☐

pig   pig   pig

☐☐☐☐   ☐☐☐☐   ☐☐☐☐

rat   get   pig ☐

d m u r e g

Oral trace read

red   red   red
☐☐☐☐ ☐☐☐☐ ☐☐☐☐

dog   dog   dog
☐☐☐☐ ☐☐☐☐ ☐☐☐☐

mud   mud   mud
☐☐☐☐ ☐☐☐☐ ☐☐☐☐

red dog mud. ☐

l f   b p   i n

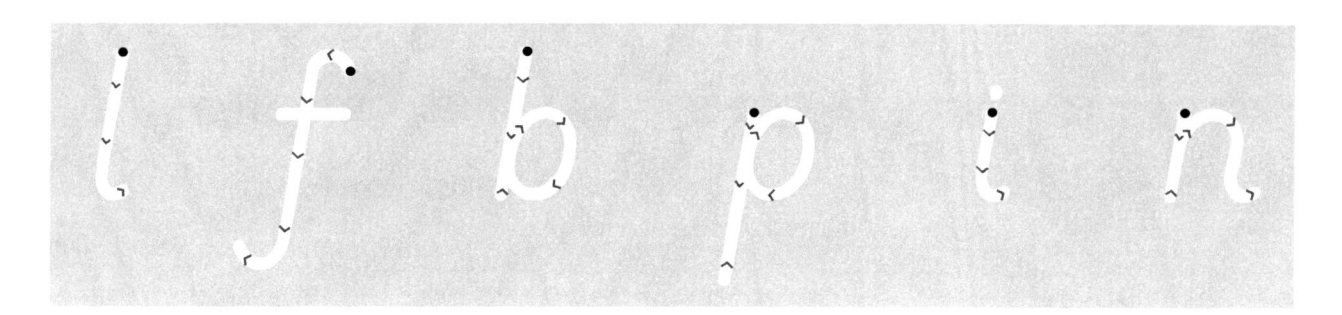

Oral | trace | read

big | big | big
☐☐☐☐ | ☐☐☐☐ | ☐☐☐☐

fun | fun | fun
☐☐☐☐ | ☐☐☐☐ | ☐☐☐☐

leg | leg | leg
☐☐☐☐ | ☐☐☐☐ | ☐☐☐☐

big   fun   leg ☐

sh j ee p o s

Using the cursor with digraphs—always reveal both letters at once.

Oral — trace — read

see see see
☐☐☐☐ ☐☐☐☐ ☐☐☐☐

shop shop shop
☐☐☐☐ ☐☐☐☐ ☐☐☐☐

jet jet jet
☐☐☐☐ ☐☐☐☐ ☐☐☐☐

see shop jet.

a r   k   z   d   p   i

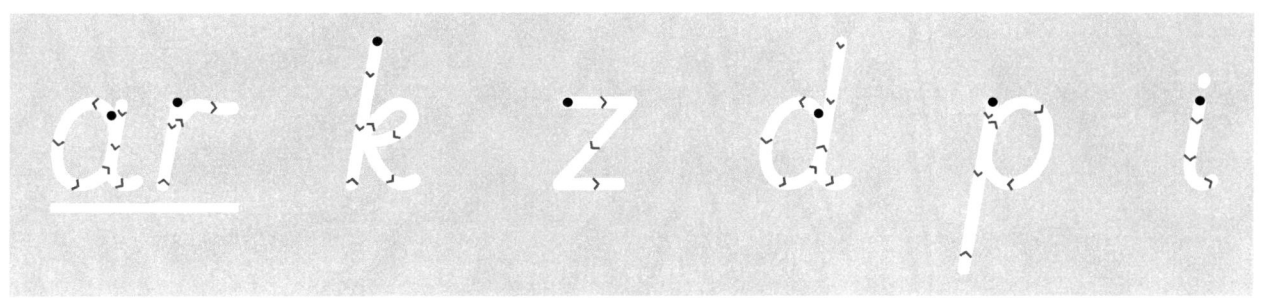

Always use the cursor!

Oral	trace	read
car	car	car
☐☐☐☐	☐☐☐☐	☐☐☐☐
kid	kid	kid
☐☐☐☐	☐☐☐☐	☐☐☐☐
zip	zip	zip
☐☐☐☐	☐☐☐☐	☐☐☐☐

car   kid   zip ☐

w x y f sh o

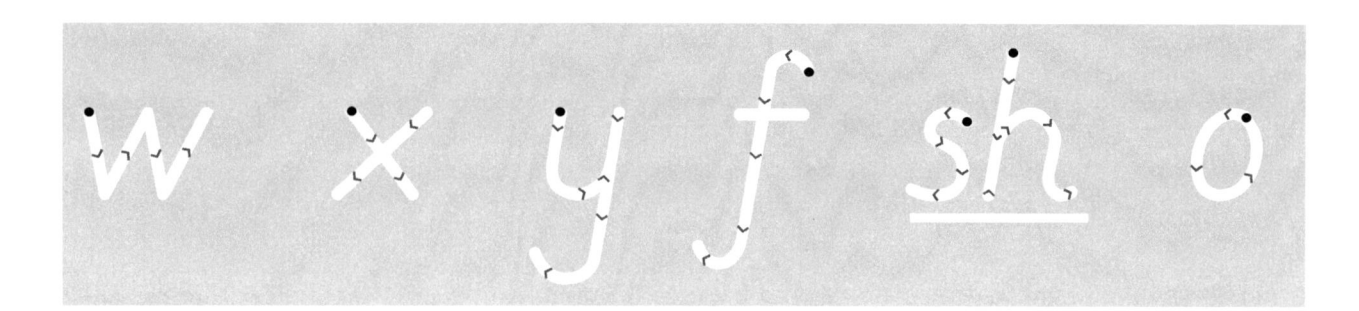

Oral   trace   read

fox   fox   fox

☐☐☐☐   ☐☐☐☐   ☐☐☐☐

yes   yes   yes

☐☐☐☐   ☐☐☐☐   ☐☐☐☐

wish   wish   wish

☐☐☐☐   ☐☐☐☐   ☐☐☐☐

fox yes wish.

v j u ee t g

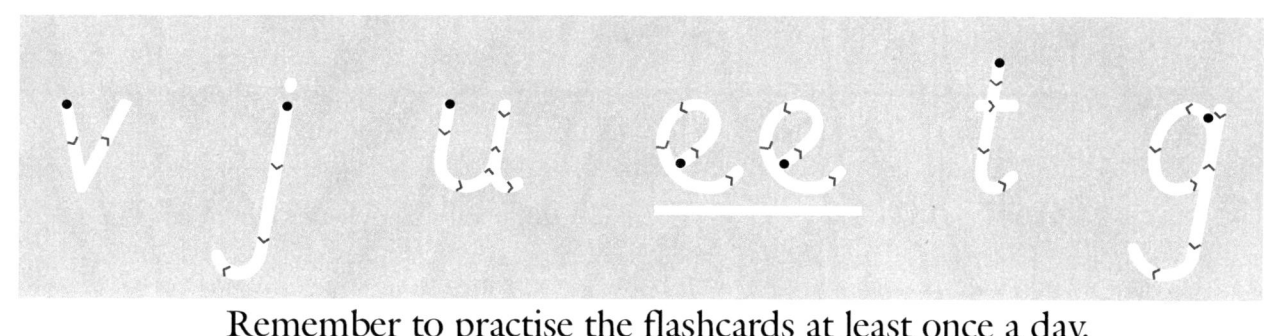

Remember to practise the flashcards at least once a day.

Oral　　　　　　　　trace　　　　　　　　read

van　　　van　　　van

☐☐☐☐　　　☐☐☐☐　　　☐☐☐☐

jug　　　jug　　　jug

☐☐☐☐　　　☐☐☐☐　　　☐☐☐☐

meet　　　meet　　　meet

☐☐☐☐　　　☐☐☐☐　　　☐☐☐☐

van jug meet ☐

dancing bears   Level 1:

Don't forget to do the flashcards at least once a day!

Pupils who can read simple words should start here.

Decoding Power Pages:

These exercises are the 'secret ingredient' of **dancing bears**. All good readers can decode letters to sound, even if they have never seen the word before. This is how good readers learn new words.

When children read the words on the Decoding Power Pages, they should not be trying to find a 'match' with a word they know. Just tell them that their job is to put the sounds together.

All the words on Decoding Power Pages are regular—they can all be 'sounded out' without any guesswork.

Remember—you must always use the cursor. You must teach pupils to scan from left to right, and to read every letter.

To earn a tick, the pupil must get all four words on a line right the first time. You may back up the cursor and tell the child to 'try again', but you cannot give any hints or prompts.

If pupils do not get the word right away, say the sounds yourself, and let them say the word. If pupils are in a total muddle, just tell them the word. Then go back to it—see The Flashback technique on page 10.

DECODING ⚡ POWER ⚡ PAGE

Always use the cursor!

gut	egg	jet	cop	☐
sell	leg	hog	van	☐
mop	hen	nod	lip	☐
pit	off	bug	cab	☐
hot	till	job	men	☐
pin	set	can	tell	☐
did	mess	puff	kill	☐
has	yet	box	gun	☐
cut	bit	beg	cat	☐
dot	fog	sub	jazz	☐

Multi-sensory 'boxes'—First, pupils trace the letters, saying the sound (or word) as they write it. Next, pupils read what they have traced.

| ee   ar   sh |

Using the cursor with digraphs—always reveal both letters at once.

s<u>ee</u>   s<u>ee</u>m   c<u>ar</u>   c<u>ar</u>t   ☐

<u>sh</u>op   wi<u>sh</u>   m<u>ee</u>t   n<u>ee</u>d   ☐

h<u>ar</u>d   di<u>sh</u>   p<u>ar</u>k   k<u>ee</u>p   ☐

| I   the   I   the |

Pupils must read the sentence, trace it, and then read it again.
They must say the words as they trace them.

I can see the car.   ☐

I need the big box.   ☐

Can I keep it?   ☐

30

> ee   ar   sh

Remember to practise the flashcards at least once a day.

see	seen	car	card	☐
ship	fish	been	feet	☐
hard	deep	part	keep	☐

> I   the   I   the

I wish I had a cat. ☐

Max is in the shop. ☐

I will get the dog. ☐

Will I meet him? ☐

Jim can keep a fish. ☐

Can I see the card? ☐

ee   ar   sh   th

Do not award ticks for a 'good try'—your pupil will pay for it later!

bar		barn		wi<u>th</u>		<u>th</u>is		☐

week		feed		<u>th</u>at		dark		☐

shut		Mark		shark		dish		☐

me you the me you the

Will you sit with me?		☐

Can you get that mop?		☐

Mark has a red car.		☐

I will get that dish.		☐

Did you feed this shark?		☐

32

DECODING POWER PAGE

lot	vat	hill	lass	☐
see	seem	car	cart	☐
net	tax	ham	fit	☐
sat	jug	zap	met	☐
jam	pig	hut	tub	☐
shop	wish	meet	need	☐
six	tug	dad	zip	☐
gas	kiss	hum	miss	☐
hard	dish	park	keep	☐
fat	hit	dug	fin	☐

the you I

(Read only. If the pupil reads the sentence slowly, have him read it again.)

This is Tim. ☐

Tim is a cop. ☐

Can you see Tim? ☐

Yes, I can see Tim. ☐

Tim is a dim cop! ☐

Tim has a big dog. ☐

Max is his dog. ☐

This is the cop car. ☐

Will you sit with Max? ☐

Will Tim sit with me? ☐

DECODING ⚡ POWER ⚡ PAGE

mat	bed	tag	log	☐
this	ship	barn	seem	☐
map	sip	boss	fix	☐
mud	tap	sum	big	☐
with	far	dish	feed	☐
fox	tan	get	nut	☐
pill	tip	dog	pop	☐
bud	ran	pub	lit	☐
that	card	weed	mash	☐
bet	yell	bat	mum	☐

ar th ck

Do not award ticks for a 'good try'—your pupil will pay for it later!

far	farm	Ja<u>ck</u>	du<u>ck</u>	☐
bath	teeth	thi<u>ck</u>	this	☐
path	Mi<u>ck</u>	shark	sharp	☐

he she he she

Did she see me? ☐
Did she see me?

Will he kiss this duck? ☐
Will he kiss this duck?

Did you run up the path? ☐

Jack got in the bath. ☐

That shark has sharp teeth. ☐

36

> she he you

(Read only. If the pupil reads the sentence slowly, have him read it again.)

Jack has a sheep farm. ☐

Can you see his sheep? ☐

He keeps his sheep in the barn. ☐

Jess has a fish shop. ☐

She will sell me a fish. ☐

Will she kiss this fish? ☐

This car will not run. ☐

Can Ben fix this car? ☐

He can park the car in the barn. ☐

Did Mick feed the shark? ☐

DECODING POWER PAGE

rod	box	cot	bill	☐
then	Mark	teeth	shark	☐
top	rat	lap	rip	☐
jog	nap	rut	dip	☐
fan	fuzz	bus	doll	☐
rush	path	far	thin	☐
hid	pin	not	hat	☐
posh	card	sheep	part	☐
dig	bag	lad	mid	☐
kid	pan	hop	let	☐

Mastery Test

Any pupil who does not pass this test must go back to page 29. This is very important—a child who is struggling will not be learning. Contrary to what you would think, children do not mind going back. It's better than getting things wrong.

If the pupil needs to go back, use a different coloured pencil for the tracing exercises and for ticking the boxes.

Timed reading: 'Pass' mark is 15 seconds per line.

leg	kid	mix	fun	☐
wet	van	job	yes	☐
rag	fox	zip	cat	☐

Reading accuracy: Pass mark is one mistake.
Do not prompt. You may allow the pupil to self correct, but you cannot say anything except "Try again".

Can you see the car? ☐

She has sharp teeth. ☐

Will he get a job? ☐

I wish I had a dog. ☐

Did Max need a bath? ☐

DECODING POWER PAGE

bad	hip	kin	yes	☐
bee	shop	car	wish	☐
bell	him	less	fed	☐
web	cup	fuss	ebb	☐
back	thick	lock	neck	☐
ken	pun	wed	bill	☐
need	farm	meet	dark	☐
luck	than	Beth	pack	☐
hiss	Ben	ell	kit	☐
rap	wig	boff	huss	☐

er ck th

her	herd	Beth	Jack	☐
duck	Vern	sick	that	☐
kerb	Herb	thin	nerd	☐

my why my why

Beth has a herd of sheep. ☐

Will you tell my dad? ☐

Why is Jack sick? ☐

Vern sat on the kerb. ☐

Herb will get my duck. ☐

Has Bert fed my pig? ☐

Why did you kiss that nerd? ☐

DECODING POWER PAGE

Do not award ticks for a 'good try'—your pupil will pay for it later!

ship	keep	see	cash	☐
mix	ted	bid	fen	☐
jerk	that	tick	duck	☐
week	rush	bark	sheep	☐
bib	fad	luff	Jess	☐
herd	than	with	nerd	☐
hard	posh	been	sham	☐
wax	moss	con	got	☐
back	deck	thin	Herb	☐
part	mash	deep	far	☐

dancing bears

Cloze Sentences:

Pupils enjoy these exercises, and they get to practise using the words they have learnt by reading them in meaningful sentences.

Sight words:

In the box at the top of each page, you will find the sight words that the pupil will need in order to read the sentences. Ask the pupil to read them—tell him the correct response if he does not know it. Use the cursor, but reveal the entire word at once. Using the Flashback Technique (see page 10), repeat each word until firm.

Reading the sentences:

Cover the sentence and ask the pupil to read the three 'answer' words underneath the sentence first, using the cursor as usual. (This prevents him guessing at what he thinks must be the missing word.) Then let the pupil read the sentence, still using the cursor. If the pupil reads the sentence and selects the right answer without prompting, allow him to circle the correct word. Otherwise, the sentence should be repeated in a subsequent lesson. If the pupil does not know the meaning of a word, explain it as simply as possible—but in no circumstances encourage pupils to 'guess' at words they have read incorrectly.

> I he she me we be

I am in a ___.

        hen   bat   van

We will sit on a ___.

        jug   rug   bell

She did not let me get a ___.

        pet   hop   lit

He did not tell his ___.

        hat   cup   dad

Did he miss his ___?

        dud   dad   did

Can a fat man dig a big ___?

        jug   hill   pit

ee ar sh

hard	feel	farm	dish	☐
Bart	mash	yard	weeds	☐
shark	seeds	Josh	seen	☐

my why my why

Why is that shark sad? ☐

Has she seen my seeds? ☐

Bart has hit her car. ☐

I will cut the weeds in the yard. ☐

Why did Josh feel sick? ☐

Shall I mix my dish of mash? ☐

We had a hard job at the farm. ☐

> said   why   by

Tim, the dim cop.

Tim the dim cop has a dog. Max is his dog. Max said, "I need a fish. A big fish on a dish. Can I get a fish?"

Tim said, "Why not? Yes, you can get a fish. A big wet fish! Jess has a fish shop. We can run by her fish shop in this car."

Tim the dim cop got in the car. Max got in the cop car. But the car did not run. Max said, "We need gas in this car!"

DECODING ~ POWER ~ PAGE

Always use the cursor!

buff	ness	bin	fib	☐
buck	sock	them	her	☐
fee	shot	feet	carp	☐
nag	teg	doff	cox	☐
bath	herb	kick	ruck	☐
dish	seem	card	lash	☐
tod	duff	will	fid	☐
puck	berth	dock	then	☐
peel	arm	shell	seed	☐
had	fell	sad	rug	☐

I he she me we be

I bet a fat dog is well ___.

       cat   fed   ham

A bad kid hit his ___.

       nod   hug   dad

She did not let me on the ___.

       bus   nut   kit

Get the dog off the ___.

       gas   bed   pin

Can you get the lid off the ___?

       bug   pig   jam

The mad dog bit the man on his ___.

       hop   leg   tub

or ch qu Qu

for	fork	quack	torch	☐
much	quit	chips	quiz	☐
rich	Queen	north	quick	☐

and why fly

The Queen has had my fish and chips. ☐

Did he get much for his car? ☐

Why did that duck quack? ☐

My dad has quit his job. ☐

You can get my torch if it is dark. ☐

We will fly up north this week. ☐

You will not get rich in this quiz. ☐

DECODING POWER PAGE

fern	moth	thick	pack	☐
quack	fork	quit	much	☐
jar	bash	lee	shin	☐
lag	rid	wit	bob	☐
verb	thug	path	wack	☐
queen	North	chock	torn	☐
heel	art	shall	park	☐
cos	god	nib	ten	☐
York	larch	quiz	porch	☐
vat	ham	met	fit	☐

Mastery Test

Any pupil who does not pass this test must go back to page 40. This is very important—a child who is struggling will not be learning. Contrary to what you would think, children do not mind going back. It's better than getting things wrong.

If the pupil needs to go back, use a different coloured pencil for the tracing exercises and for ticking the boxes.

Timed reading: 'Pass' mark is 15 seconds per line.

park	keep	this	shop	☐
with	sharp	her	sick	☐
need	will	dish	with	☐

Reading accuracy: Pass mark is one mistake.
Do not prompt. You may allow the pupil to self correct, but you cannot say anything except "Try again".

Why is she in my car? ☐

Jack said that we can sit on the bed. ☐

Tell me why you did that. ☐

Did Bart cut the weeds in the back yard? ☐

Kim has a bad rash on her neck. ☐

said to do who

The pork chop.

Tim the dim cop said, "We need to get gas. We can not get to the fish shop if we need gas. Who can get a can of gas?"

Max said, "Yes, I can do that. My pal Vern has a can. I will see Vern, and then we can get the gas." Tim the dim cop said, "Why not?"

Max ran to get his pal Vern. But then he met Herb, who had a big pork chop. Max said, "Will you sell me that pork chop?"

Will Max get the gas?

52

> you by my why try

She has not fed the ___.

    map   dog   wet

Can you cut the fat off my ___?

    boss   ham   mud

My cat will sit on my ___.

    jam   gum   lap

If you get mud on me I will ___.

    cry   hiss   quack

She has a rag doll by the ___.

    fell   tag   bed

Why did she quit her ___.

    job   jam   jar

> *er ck th*

her	Herb	them	jack	☐
perk	luck	Nick	Beth	☐
socks	Rick	Vern	this	☐

> *give have live*

Did Nick give them his socks? ☐

Do you have her torch? ☐

Herb and Beth live on a ship. ☐

Jack will perk up if she gives him a kiss. ☐

Rick has had bad luck this week. ☐

Who did Vern give my chips to? ☐

She did not give me much fish. ☐

DECODING POWER PAGE

Don't forget to do the flashcards at least once a day!

quick	rich	sort	charm	☐
Dick	kerb	Thor	Perth	☐
bar	seen	rash	darn	☐
quid	porch	quiff	forth	☐
Jack	perm	teeth	thorn	☐
cuff	bod	hem	nub	☐
worn	chap	quin	nor	☐
tern	pith	lick	chuck	☐
feed	cart	shun	mark	☐
lot	zap	tax	tub	☐

55

> *by my why try fly*

Can I try on the red ___?

      pig   hat   mug

My dog will sit by ___.

      me   in   up

Can you fill my ___?

      dog   nap   cup

Will you fly in a ___?

      bee   jet   hen

Why is she in ___?

      log   pan   bed

Will the hen let me get an ___?

      egg   sun   box

or ay oy				

t<u>oy</u>	h<u>ay</u>	b<u>oy</u>	m<u>ay</u>	☐
p<u>ay</u>	R<u>oy</u>	R<u>ay</u>	torch	☐
s<u>ay</u>	short	w<u>ay</u>	s<u>oy</u>	☐

to do give have

May we feed the hay to the sheep? ☐

This path is the way to the farm. ☐

Roy gave his toys to Vern. ☐

Can you give me that jar of soy? ☐

Who will pay for my fish and chips? ☐

Why did the boy say that? ☐

Do you need a torch to see in the dark? ☐

are so no go

Max's shorts.

Herb said to Max, "Why yes, I will sell you this pork chop. Give me six rats and you can have it."

Max said, "I do not have six rats, but I can give you my shorts. I have had a bath this week, so my shorts are not so bad."

Herb said, "I do not need the shorts. But you are a dog, so you can get six rats. Then you can have this pork chop."

Do you need six rats?

DECODING POWER PAGE

Do not award ticks for a 'good try'—your pupil will pay for it later!

weep	shim	weed	darn	☐
boy	say	day	joy	☐
goth	hers	shock	them	☐
tort	quill	perch	chub	☐
Roy	pay	toy	lay	☐
posh	lard	beet	marsh	☐
berg	hack	perk	thorn	☐
coy	soy	may	ray	☐
chick	quell	torch	ford	☐
hill	lass	net	jug	☐

> my why try fly cry

You can cut a bit off my ___.

  dog dad ham

Do not let the dog lay on the ___.

  boy bed Queen

Why will he cry if we hit ___?

  him fog hop

Can you rip the top off the ___?

  yell box bed

You can fly if you ___.

  hop yell try

Why did Dad sell his red ___?

  mess rip van

> *or qu ai*

l<u>ai</u>d	corn	quit	G<u>ai</u>l	☐
p<u>ai</u>d	f<u>ai</u>l	for	r<u>ai</u>n	☐
Queen	Norm	w<u>ai</u>t	quick	☐

> *to + day = today*
> *for + got = forgot*
> *can + not = cannot*

Pupils trace these word sums and then read them. Explain what they have to do, but do not award a tick unless they can read all of the words without prompting.

Has the Queen paid for her corn? ☐

That hen laid an egg today. ☐

I forgot to pay for my toys. ☐

Why did Norm quit his job at the jail? ☐

Gail cannot wait for her bus today. ☐

If you are quick, you can sit by the Queen. ☐

Mastery Test

Any pupil who does not pass this test must go back to page 52. This is very important—a child who is struggling will not be learning. Contrary to what you would think, children do not mind going back. It's better than getting things wrong.

If the pupil needs to go back, use a different coloured pencil for the tracing exercises and for ticking the boxes.

Timed reading: 'Pass' mark is 15 seconds per line.

boy	torch	Beth	quit	☐
say	queen	fork	chop	☐
way	much	luck	north	☐

Reading accuracy: Pass mark is one mistake.

Do not prompt. You may allow the pupil to self correct, but you cannot say anything except "Try again".

I forgot to give my toys to Mark. ☐

If you are quick, you may feed the shark. ☐

Do you have to pay for the fish and chips? ☐

Roy had to go to the farm in the dark. ☐

Why did you pay so much for that lock? ☐

dancing bears

Well done!

you have completed
Level 1

You are now working on Level 2.

dancing bears   Level 2:

Gail had a pail of cat's tails.

65

to do are to do are

Six rats.

Max had to get six rats to pay for Herb's pork chop. Then he met Gail, who had a pail of cat's tails. Max said, "I need to get six rats. Do you have six rats?"

Gail said, "No, but six rats live in Norm's barn. Tim, Kim and Jim are short rats with fat tails. Ben, Ken and Len are fat rats with short tails."

Max said, "If this is the road to Norm's barn, I can get the rats. Then I can pay for Herb's pork chop!"

Do you have a short tail?

DECODING POWER PAGE

Always use the cursor!

say	pail	main	joy	☐
horse	parch	norm	quip	☐
rack	verse	lath	thud	☐
paid	path	lain	hay	☐
arch	form	quiff	morse	☐
ash	eel	mesh	reed	☐
way	maid	fail	coy	☐
quin	orb	leech	fort	☐
Bert	nerve	hock	thick	☐
jam	tug	hum	log	☐

> so are to do who

Why is it hot in the ___?

      sun   beg   dot

I will cry if you will not let me sit by my ___.

      bill   dad   zap

I wish I had a ___.

      car   hid   heel

The seeds are in the ___.

      sheep   jar   fish

Do not hit him so ___.

      carp   art   hard

Who shall we feed to the ___?

      ship   shop   shark

oi oa ch

l<u>oa</u>d	<u>oi</u>l	Chuck	c<u>oa</u>t	☐
l<u>oa</u>n	j<u>oi</u>n	J<u>oa</u>n	b<u>oi</u>l	☐
c<u>oi</u>n	l<u>oa</u>f	b<u>oa</u>t	lunch	☐

who do
sail + boat = sailboat

Will you join us for a quick lunch? ☐

Did you see who got my coat? ☐

Chuck's car needs gas and oil. ☐

That is not the way to load a gun. ☐

Joan can boil the chips in oil. ☐

Who will join me on my sailboat? ☐

If you loan me the coins, I will get a loaf. ☐

DECODING POWER PAGE

Don't forget to do the flashcards at least once a day!

vain	soap	coin	bay	☐
pig	meet	zip	shop	☐
lark	jeep	harsh	shut	☐
foil	goal	may	Roy	☐
hut	need	six	kiss	☐
pert	mock	terse	chock	☐
fail	coach	pay	toil	☐
dad	gas	dish	tag	☐
cord	beech	quack	march	☐
miss	park	bed	keep	☐

no go so are to do who

Will we go in the ___?

    bee   car   wish

Did she shut up the ___?

    seem   bark   shop

I had a red rash on my ___.

    arm   ship   see

I keep my pet fish in a ___.

    heel   shut   jar

Can you see who is in the ___?

    sheep   dish   car

Do not get the sheet off the ___.

    bat   bar   bed

was are was are

Ken, the tin rat.

Max ran up the road to Norm's barn. Then he met Ken. Ken was a toy rat. Max said, "Who are you? You are not a fat rat with a short tail."

Ken said, "No, I am a tin rat. I am Ken, the tin rat. I live with Jill, my pet toad. She will boil the oil, and then we can have lunch."

"But Gail said that six rats live in Norm's barn," Max said. I cannot see Len and Ben, nor do I see Tim, Kim or Jim."

Ken said, "Len and Ben had to go to get the soap for Bill the goat. Tim, Kim and Jim had to go with them. Did you see them go in the sailboat?"

Do you wish you had a pet toad?

DECODING POWER PAGE

hard	mat	cart	boss	☐
coal	lay	nail	quoin	☐
harp	dosh	seep	par	☐
fix	with	barn	tap	☐
coil	oak	Tay	waif	☐
therm	serve	lock	wick	☐
sum	dish	fox	mash	☐
oil	poach	soy	lain	☐
shorn	Norse	cheek	quid	☐
mat	ship	feed	tag	☐

no go so are to do who

Did he try to reel in the big ___?

    dish   fish   feet

Has she been on a ___?

    bash   bee   ship

Who can feed the ___?

    sheep   cash   bar

Did my dog bark at the ___?

    fee   ash   car

I cut my shin on a sharp ___.

    shell   char   feed

Why has the cat got mud on his ___?

    jar   feet   shut

> ay oi oy ay oi oy

rain	Roy	lay	paid
way	wait	Kay	boy
toy	Gail	sail	say

> tin + foil = tinfoil
> sail + boat = sailboat

Kay and the boys are on the way to the jail. ☐

If it rains, her coat will get wet. ☐

Why did Roy wait for the coach? ☐

My goat had tinfoil for lunch. ☐

My dad got me a toy sailboat. ☐

Did Gail say who has the soap? ☐

If you lay in bed today, you will not get paid. ☐

Mastery Test

Any pupil who does not pass this test must go back to page 65. This is very important—a child who is struggling will not be learning. Contrary to what you would think, children do not mind going back. It's better than getting things wrong.

If the pupil needs to go back, use a different coloured pencil for the tracing exercises and for ticking the boxes.

Timed reading: 'Pass' mark is 15 seconds per line.

wait	road	sail	corn	☐
rack	join	boat	rain	☐
tail	oil	path	Vern	☐

Reading accuracy: Pass mark is one mistake.

Do not prompt. You may allow the pupil to self correct, but you cannot say anything except "Try again".

Did you see who paid for the coach? ☐

Get the soap and have a soak in the bath. ☐

Gail's pet goat had to wait for her lunch. ☐

Will you loan me a coin for my chips? ☐

Norm will join us for a run in the park. ☐

Advanced Flashcards:

The advanced flashcards are printed on blue card. They should be cut up and used in just the same way as the basic flashcards. You should note that many of these cards represent two phonemes (eg, 'oke & ake'), but you will model these without breaking them down.

This is the first introduction to the silent 'e' rule. You need not go into it at this stage, but it helps them get used to the spelling pattern. In any case, it is always best to keep the rules to a minimum—especially with young children.

Final Consonant Blends:

Most children master consonant blends easily, but in some cases this can be a serious problem. If your pupil is having trouble, you will find the following sheets of final consonant blends helpful.

You will notice that the words are arranged in pairs. The first word is a CVC word, and the second is the same word with another consonant added. The first pair is

    ten   tent

By now your pupil will be able to read 'ten' with no trouble. He should be able to add the final consonant without too much difficulty. If he cannot, you will have to do a bit of oral blending for him. For instance, say the word 'ten'—pause for a split second—and then add the final /t/. Then ask him what the word was. Obviously, you don't give him a tick until he can do this entirely on his own.

DECODING ~ POWER ~ PAGE
Final Consonant Blends

ten	tent	bus	bust	☐
tan	tank	pin	pink	☐
pass	past	loss	lost	☐
hill	hilt	ran	rant	☐
sun	sunk	chum	chump	☐
gun	gunk	sill	silk	☐
shell	shelf	hem	hemp	☐
dam	damp	hell	held	☐
Bess	best	well	Welsh	☐

they was who

No lunch for Max.

Max had to wait for the rest of the tin rats. They got back the next day. Max said, "We must go see Herb, who has a pork chop for my lunch. He said that he needs six rats."

Ken, Len and Ben went up the road with Max. So did Jim, Kim and Tim. They went up the road to see Herb. Max said, "I have six rats for you. Can I have that pork chop? I need my lunch."

Herb was mad. He said, "Why they are just tin rats. I need fat rats with short tails. I need short rats with fat tails. But I do not need toy rats."

Max said, "Then I must get Vern, who has a gas can. Then I can go with Tim, the dim cop. We can go to see Jess, who has a fish shop. Then I can have my lunch."

DECODING POWER PAGE

Always use the cursor!

bed	this	log	seem	☐
quern	thick	erse	thug	☐
bait	foam	Hoy	quail	☐
morn	queen	chard	gorse	☐
reel	marl	hash	sharp	☐
map	far	sip	thus	☐
check	herl	lack	with	☐
tail	day	foal	soil	☐
cork	chart	quiz	lord	☐
pill	ran	weed	rug	☐

> go was why to do who

Why did he shut my dog in a ___?

    heel   shed   arm

If I feel ill, who will get me a ___?

    fee   mark   pill

Who was hit by the red ___?

    car   dash   seem

Why did the man in the shop keep his cash in the ___?

    shark   feet   till

It is hard to see a car in the ___.

    dash   dark   deed

Do you need to go to the ___?

    shop   sharp   sheet

air oar eer ore

air	fair	wore	beer	☐
pair	soar	deer	score	☐
cheer	more	chair	hoard	☐

they of who

Sit in that chair and I will cut her hair. ☐

Joan wore her red dress to the fair. ☐

I will give a cheer if they score a goal. ☐

Did you see that bat soar in the air? ☐

My dad has a hoard of coins in a box. ☐

Who will get more beer for the boys? ☐

Gail wore a pair of red socks today. ☐

Final Consonant Blends

hell	help	pan	pant	☐
loss	lost	ran	rank	☐
pun	punch	well	weld	☐
bus	busk	cull	cult	☐
lass	last	miss	mist	☐
gull	gulf	gas	gasp	☐
less	lest	ten	tend	☐
gull	gulp	fun	funk	☐
mass	mask	bell	belt	☐

> some of they
> sun + day = Sunday

Joan, the big roan.

Ken the tin rat felt sad, for Max was in a bad way. Big dogs need to have lunch. Ken said, "I will loan you my horse. uoan the big roan can get you to Jess's fish shop. Then you can have lunch."

Max said, "Why, thank you. A fish on a dish will hit the spot." So Max got on Joan the big roan, and they went off to get some fish.

On the way to the fish shop, they met Tim the dim cop. Tim was in his cop car. He had to sleep in his car, and his hair was a mess.

Tim was glad to see Max. He got on Joan the big roan, and off they went to the fish shop. But they forgot that it was Sunday.

"No!" Tim said. "Jess has shut her fish shop!"
But Joan said, "Do not be so sad. I have lots of Mars bars in my nosh bag."

DECODING POWER PAGE

Do not award ticks for a 'good try'—your pupil will pay for it later!

core	leer	chair	board	☐
bust	held	jump	land	☐
Kay	foil	loath	main	☐
yank	lamp	help	dent	☐
Norm	cheep	quip	born	☐
and	dunk	lend	silk	☐
shack	verve	oath	rock	☐
fist	tank	send	cost	☐
carve	deed	gash	reef	☐
pub	weed	pill	that	☐

of have some they said

Do you keep the sheep in the yard or in the ___?

    shop   barn   feet

You need some cash to go in a ___.

    art   far   cab

Mum said I have to pick up my ___.

    pecks   socks   licks

She has a duck in her ___.

    nerd   suck   bath

Have they been to the ___?

    thick   shop   jerk

My dog will try to lick my ___.

    mark   herb   feet

Mastery Test

Any pupil who does not pass this test must go back to page 79. This is very important—a child who is struggling will not be learning. Contrary to what you would think, children do not mind going back. It's better than getting things wrong.

If the pupil needs to go back, use a different coloured pencil for the tracing exercises and for ticking the boxes.

Timed reading: 'Pass' mark is 15 seconds per line.

lost	belt	foil	quiz	☐
help	chart	pain	joy	☐
sank	herb	goat	hay	☐

Reading accuracy: Pass mark is one mistake.
Do not prompt. You may allow the pupil to self correct, but you cannot say anything except "Try again".

Have they had some of the punch? ☐

Do they have some beer on board that boat? ☐

Who can lend me a hand with this chair? ☐

Did that silk vest cost much? ☐

Faith and Vern live on the main road. ☐

dancing bears

Well done!

you have completed
Level 2

You are now working on Level 3.

dancing bears — Level 3:

Fluency Reading:

Timed readings will help your child read words quickly and automatically. At first, the times are very easy. Some children get nervous when they are being tested, and you don't want them to get worried about the stopwatch. For real timing-phobics, sit the child with his back to a wall clock with a second hand.

Frame the first word in the line with the cursor, and then say 'go'. Move the cursor as fast as the pupil can read. Record the time on the sheet, and tick the line off if the pupil reads every word within 10 seconds. The usual rules apply—if the child makes a mistake, you can move the cursor back and let him have another go, but you cannot give him any help. Model any word he gets stuck on and re-time that line the next day.

Unless the pupil is extremely slow, he will want to try for bonus points. You can award one bonus point if the pupil reads the line in 8 seconds, and two bonus points if he reads it in 6 seconds. You can get little sticky stars to stick on the sheet, or you can agree on certain rewards when he gets enough stars (eg, staying up an extra half-hour at the weekend, or a sleep-over with a friend). If the pupil wants to have a second go at a line to win a bonus point, he must wait until the following day.

Story:

The story is intended as a reward, so if the pupil wants to control the cursor, he may. (This is *never* allowed on any other page.) There is no tick-box for this exercise but if the pupil struggles with a sentence, he should be encouraged to read it again. It may be a good idea to read the story twice to improve fluency. Model any words the pupil gets stuck on.

FLUENCY READING

Timed reading:
☐ Pass: 10 sec.   ☆ Bonus: 8 sec.   ☆ Double Bonus: 6 sec.

gut	sell	mop	pit	☐ ☆ ☆
hot	pin	did	has	☐ ☆ ☆
cut	egg	leg	hen	☐ ☆ ☆
off	till	set	mess	☐ ☆ ☆
yet	bit	jet	hog	☐ ☆ ☆
nod	bug	job	can	☐ ☆ ☆
puff	box	beg	cop	☐ ☆ ☆
van	lip	cab	men	☐ ☆ ☆
tell	kill	gun	cat	☐ ☆ ☆

was here

On the way to the shop.

Mark was lost. His mum had sent him to get a loaf and milk for lunch. He went up the road to the shop, and then he met Vern. Vern was a big boy and he had a pet snail. "You must meet my snail", Vern said. "Froid is my pet snail. He just had beer and roast beef for lunch. See him sit in his chair and rest".

Vern let Mark pick up Froid, who was Vern's pet snail. Vern let Mark pick up his chair. "Froid has wet feet", said Mark. Vern said, "Why, yes, Froid is a snail!"

Next, we will tell you why Mark got lost.

DECODING POWER PAGE

kip	null	yam	bun	☐
mink	weld	risk	past	☐
hair	fore	peer	boar	☐
ant	sing	fond	daft	☐
Joan	aim	roach	fay	☐
barn	lush	sash	seek	☐
pong	imp	lunch	went	☐
nick	kerf	term	thug	☐
worn	quench	chill	port	☐
sung	punch	belt	end	☐

of have some they said

Can he pick up that ___?

    rock   than   herd

They have some fish in that ___.

    luck   fern   shop

Do not run on the deck with wet ___.

    peck   feet   this

They can go in my ___.

    with   car   seem

Can a bee fly as far as a ___?

    moth   herd   sock

Some of us will go to the ___.

    pick   perk   park

| oi air eer ore |

joint   pair   more   deer ☐

chair   queer   point   tore ☐

moist   wore   cheer   hair ☐

| where here there |

We need some more chairs here. ☐

The coat she wore is moist with the rain. ☐

There are six deer in the park. ☐

Where did you get that pair of red socks? ☐

Can you point to the boy who tore his vest? ☐

You can sit in the chair if you feel a bit queer. ☐

There are six joints of pork left. ☐

FLUENCY READING

Timed reading:
☐ Pass: 10 sec.   ☆ Bonus: 8 sec.   ★ Double Bonus: 6 sec.

dot	lot	net	sat	☐ ☆ ★
jam	six	gas	wax	☐ ☆ ★
dug	fog	vat	tax	☐ ☆ ★
jug	pig	tug	kiss	☐ ☆ ★
hit	got	sub	hill	☐ ☆ ★
ham	zap	hut	dad	☐ ☆ ★
hum	fat	had	jazz	☐ ☆ ★
lass	fit	met	tub	☐ ☆ ★
zip	miss	hex	fin	☐ ☆ ★

Off to the tip.

Mark let Vern have his pet snail back. Froid the snail just sat in his chair and Vern let him rest. Vern said, "You must go to the tip with me. We can have lots of fun at the tip." Mark said, "But I must go to the shop and get a loaf and some milk for my lunch. Mum will be mad if I am not back". Vern said, "It will be quick if we fly. You can fly if you try!"

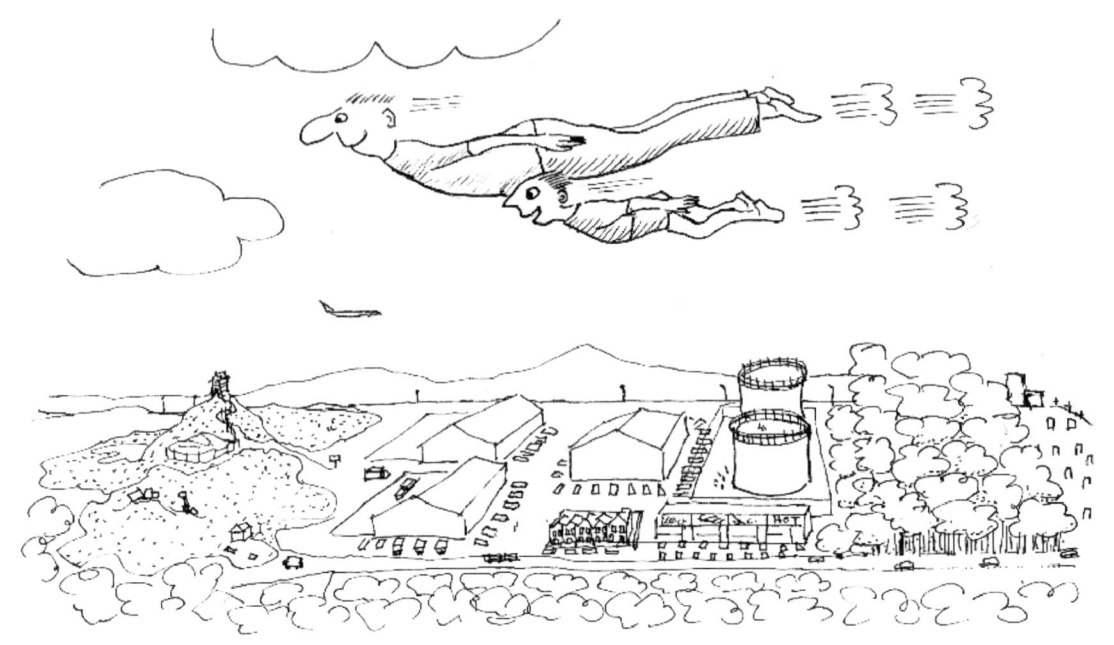

So Mark and Vern set off to fly to the tip. They got to the tip with Froid, the pet snail. The tip was big and it was full of junk. It had a pong of damp dog. "We can have lots of fun in that hill of moist muck!" said Vern.

Can you think why Mark got lost?

DECODING POWER PAGE

Always use the cursor!

jail	soy	oat	quoit	☐
beer	more	fair	roar	☐
born	quilt	chip	for	☐
moist	wimp	hang	fact	☐
verve	teem	mush	hark	☐
shore	fair	board	deer	☐
chimp	bung	ramp	pink	☐
huff	bell	odd	lax	☐
think	erne	muck	chick	☐
serf	thank	pick	perch	☐

of have some they here

Nan said not to let the cat lick the ___.

        kerb   dish   luck

She said she has had bad luck this ___.

        pith   duck   week

Do you feel ___?

        sock   seek   sick

They will have to rush to get back here by ___.
        duck   six   pith

They hid some of the cash in a box with a ___.

        lick   lack   lock

Can you serve me with some thin cut ___?

        hat   ham   hop

oar ai oa

boar	board	faith	foam	☐
quail	oak	sail	oars	☐
soap	train	coarse	boat	☐

card + board = cardboard
was here where

My toy train is here in this cardboard box. ☐

Mix that soap, and it will foam up. ☐

A boar is a pig that has tusks. ☐

Where was the sailboat today? ☐

Do goats have coarse hair? ☐

Here is an oak board that will do for a shelf. ☐

The boat will not go if you forget the oars. ☐

FLUENCY READING

Timed reading:
☐ Pass: 10 sec.   ☆ Bonus: 8 sec.   ★ Double Bonus: 6 sec.

mat	map	mud	fox	☐ ☆ ★
pill	bud	bet	dux	☐ ☆ ★
kid	bed	sip	tap	☐ ☆ ★
tan	tip	ran	yell	☐ ☆ ★
fell	pan	tag	boss	☐ ☆ ★

Bart, the Junk-yard dog.

So Mark, Vern and Froid went to the hill of moist muck. Froid was just a short snail, so he had to go. Then they met Bart, the junk-yard dog. Bart had the pong of a damp dog. But then Bart *was* a damp dog. Bart said, "Will you join me for some roast toad? I have a pair of hot toads in my hill of moist muck."

Vern said, "Froid can not have roast toad for he is a snail. Can we have a short shark?" Bart said, "The last short shark went off to see the queen. But you can have a sharp shark." Mark said, "Thank you so much, but I must tell my mum or she will be mad."

Next, you will see why Mark did not get his lunch.

DECODING POWER PAGE

joint	kiln	dump	song	☐
sore	pair	jeer	soar	☐
yarn	gosh	feel	teen	☐
chop	bort	quill	pork	☐
zest	gasp	melt	chink	☐
ore	lair	queer	roar	☐
win	gaff	Max	rig	☐
ring	quest	pelt	jilt	☐
load	coy	quail	void	☐
say	her	quill	coin	☐

> here where there

Can a duck ___?

    quit   quick   quack

A shark has a lot of sharp ___.

    teem   thick   teeth

A rich man has a lot of ___.

    quiz   card   cash

You can sit here on this ___.

    mat   mug   mop

Do they have much ___?

    cash   chill   chuck

There are a lot of fish on my ___.

    cheek   dish   chin

FLUENCY READING

Timed reading:
☐ Pass: 10 sec. ☆ Bonus: 8 sec. ★ Double Bonus: 6 sec.

sum	get	dog	pub	☐ ☆ ★
bat	sad	hop	log	☐ ☆ ★
fix	big	nut	pop	☐ ☆ ★
lit	mum	rug	let	☐ ☆ ★
rod	top	jog	fan	☐ ☆ ★

> here where

Shark oil.

Mark went with Vern, Froid and Bart to the deep pond, where they met Herb. Herb was the sharp shark. "I am glad you are here for lunch," he said. "My back is sore and I need some oil. Here is ten quid for some oil." Bart said, "There are lots of junk cars here. I can go and drain some oil, then we can boil a joint of beef. I will bark if I get lost."

Then Froid fell off his chair in to some moist muck. Vern said, "Can you see where Froid went?" Mark said, "Yes, he is in his shell. Shall I go and get my loaf and some milk?" But Bart was not back with the oil, so they had to ask Herb to wait in the deep pond. It was dark in his shell, so Froid went to sleep. "Who will tell my mum where I am?" Asked Mark.

Do you think Mark's mum was mad?

Mastery Test

Any pupil who does not pass this test must go back to page 94. This is very important—a child who is struggling will not be learning. Contrary to what you would think, children do not mind going back. It's better than getting things wrong.

If the pupil needs to go back, use a different coloured pencil for the tracing exercises and for ticking the boxes.

Timed reading: 'Pass' mark is 15 seconds per line.

more	bunch	coil	porch	☐
fair	damp	moat	kerb	☐
beer	melt	quail	point	☐

Reading accuracy: Pass mark is one mistake.

Do not prompt. You may allow the pupil to self correct, but you cannot say anything except "Try again".

Did you see where the sailboat went? ☐

A cardboard box will not keep you dry in a hard rain. ☐

Who was the boy in the torn coat? ☐

The coach to Perth will be here on Sunday. ☐

Is there no more of that beef joint left? ☐

DECODING POWER PAGE
Initial Consonant Blends

stop	play	flag	☐
drop	glad	swim	☐
grab	spell	slip	☐
brick	clay	trick	☐
skill	black	crab	☐
frog	pram	twin	☐
snap	dwell	smug	☐
skim	Gwen	twill	☐

DECODING POWER PAGE

Don't forget to do the flashcards at least once a day!

bunch	elf	foist	bang	☐
frog	twin	still	snap	☐
oat	rail	hoist	bay	☐
clock	flag	pram	swim	☐
quell	horn	char	cord	☐
blot	droll	flock	grit	☐
lung	chunk	act	vest	☐
twill	slop	green	crab	☐
sheer	bore	fair	oar	☐
pail	quip	horse	joy	☐

> here where there

There are ten ducks in the ___.

      luck   term   park

Shut the dog in the ___.

      porch   pick   port

Can I dig here with my ___?

      pork   fork   ford

Where is my big, fat pork ___?

      cord   quell   chop

They had some fish and ___.

      chins   chips   chills

You can see in the dark if you have a ___.

      fork   port   torch

FLUENCY READING

Timed reading:
☐Pass: 10 sec.　☆Bonus: 8 sec.　★Double Bonus: 6 sec.

hid	dig	bad	bell	☐ ☆ ★
hug	box	rat	nap	☐ ☆ ★
fuzz	pin	bag	hip	☐ ☆ ★
him	pot	cot	lap	☐ ☆ ★
rut	bus	not	lad	☐ ☆ ★

A crock of eels.

Mark and Vern left the deep pond to see where Bart had got to. Bart was a damp dog and damp dogs smell, so Mark and Vern just had to sniff. Herb the sharp shark had to stay in the deep pond, for he did not have a bus pass. Froid was still stuck in the moist muck, yet he still did not have his chair.

"I can smell a strong pong," said Vern, "so Bart must be here." But Bart was not here and he was not there. Mark said, "Here is a crock of eels. They smell a lot. They must be the things we can smell." Vern said, "Ask that eel if he has seen Bart the junk-yard dog." But the eel did not say where Bart was. He just swam in his crock and stank. Mark said, "I must get back or my mum will tell the cops that I am lost."

Do you think that Mark was lost?

Initial Consonant Blends

fleet	storm	sleep	start	train	☐
float	creep	spoil	trail	dress	☐
swim	Fred	bleed	play	clock	☐

saw   come   put
a + way = away
be + fore = before

I think Joan snores in her sleep. ☐

We saw them start off up the trail at six o'clock. ☐

Come here and play with my toy train. ☐

You will spoil that dress if you bleed on it. ☐

Put the toys away and go to sleep. ☐

I saw Fred creep up on the deer. ☐

You must swim back to shore before the storm. ☐

DECODING ~ POWER ~ PAGE

prim	grab	drill	blob	☐
teeth	hush	chard	shark	☐
skid	glut	fled	class	☐
tuck	perch	maths	neck	☐
chat	ford	tore	quick	☐
clink	bluff	grass	plan	☐
moan	play	gait	coil	☐
lore	pair	oar	seer	☐
tuft	silk	ask	hump	☐
parch	fail	leech	hock	☐

> here where there

Where is the path to the ___?

    shop   short   such

The queen was not born in a ___.

    chop   torn   barn

She has torn her ___.

    sort   sock   such

Try not to jab me with that sharp ___.

    fort   form   fork

I put my toy duck and some soap in the ___.

    bed   chair   bath

Come here and join us for a ___.

    chat   chain   cheek

FLUENCY READING

Timed reading:
☐ Pass: 10 sec. ☆ Bonus: 8 sec. ☆ Double Bonus: 6 sec.

kin	less	cup	bill	☐ ☆ ☆
rip	dip	doll	hat	☐ ☆ ☆
mid	yes	fed	gum	☐ ☆ ☆
add	bee	web	ken	☐ ☆ ☆
need	hiss	rap	ship	☐ ☆ ☆
dud	shop	rudd	pun	☐ ☆ ☆

Groin, the gray-green goat.

Who do you think Mark and Vern ran in to on the way to the hill of moist muck? They met Groin, the gray-green goat, who wore his hair in a quiff. Vern said, "My pal Mark needs to get a loaf and some milk for his mum. Is there a store in this dump?"

Groin bit a chunk of brick and had a munch on some foil. Then he said, "You must ask Bart, the damp dog. I just have my lunch here."

Mark said, "We must go back to the deep pond and get Froid, the short snail. He must miss his chair." Groin, the gray-green goat said, "You must not trust Herb, the sharp shark, for he has no bus pass." So Vern paid Groin six coins for his torch and they went back on the trail to the deep pond.

Where do you think Bart the junk-yard dog was?

DECODING POWER PAGE

crack	drip	glass	swig	☐
woad	joint	stay	laid	☐
chuck	verse	kith	peck	☐
grip	flop	clam	skill	☐
torch	corm	cheep	quit	☐
tart	josh	yard	beef	☐
pang	mend	nest	film	☐
more	beer	Claire	hoard	☐
loach	hay	loin	Cain	☐
punch	soy	quilt	long	☐

saw   come   put   live   give

Where did you put my ___?

      cab   coat   coy

They will go to the fun-fair by ___.

      coal   coat   coach

Come and see the boat with the red ___.

      say   soil   sail

The sick boy lay on the ___.

      bay   bed   boil

We saw a goat at the ___.

      foam   farm   fail

Have you paid the man for the ___?

      laid   void   loaf

Mastery Test

Any pupil who does not pass this test must go back to page 111. This is very important—a child who is struggling will not be learning. Contrary to what you would think, children do not mind going back. It's better than getting things wrong.

If the pupil needs to go back, use a different coloured pencil for the tracing exercises and for ticking the boxes.

Timed reading: 'Pass' mark is 15 seconds per line.

spoil	store	green	black	☐
train	fair	free	play	☐
sweet	roar	smart	croak	☐

Reading accuracy: Pass mark is one mistake.

Do not prompt. You may allow the pupil to self correct, but you cannot say anything except "Try again".

Come here and we can play with the clay. ☐

The stern is the back end of a ship. ☐

Where shall I put the green sweets? ☐

They saw us put the toys by the stairs. ☐

We will try to get there before the storm ☐
  comes.

FLUENCY READING

Timed reading:
☐ Pass: 10 sec.   ☆ Bonus: 8 sec.   ⭐ Double Bonus: 6 sec.

farm	Ben	wig	rid	☐ ☆ ⭐
keep	gig	jut	car	☐ ☆ ⭐
fuss	wed	meet	ell	☐ ☆ ⭐
boff	see	mix	pug	☐ ☆ ⭐
wish	ebb	biff	dark	☐ ☆ ⭐
kit	huss	cash	Ted	☐ ☆ ⭐

Mark and the shard.

Mark and Vern left Groin the gray-green goat, who wore his hair in a quiff, and went off on the trail to the deep pond. On the way, Mark slid on some slick clay. He fell on a shard of glass and cut his arm.

Vern said, "I will put some mud on the cut so it will not bleed. It is not a bad cut, and I think you will live." Then they saw a damp dog come up the hill. "It must be Bart", said Mark, "I can tell by the smell."

Bart said, "I live in that smart shack on the steep hill. Come up the stairs with me and I will give you some lunch." But then Mark saw Froid, the short snail. He had green paint on his shell. He was still stuck in the moist muck.

Do you think Mark got his lunch?

DECODING POWER PAGE

Always use the cursor!

king	aft	bank	champ	☐
norm	chit	quilt	inch	☐
twig	fret	snip	plum	☐
Ark	meek	short	tosh	☐
elm	dung	mist	quench	☐
verse	sack	berth	luck	☐
flap	drop	bran	stab	☐
sheer	core	fair	boar	☐
foil	goad	boy	ail	☐
shelf	rung	pond	mint	☐

saw come put live give

If you are bad, you may be put in ___.

      jail   join   jay

The boy will moan if he is in ___.

      pail   poach   pain

He said that he can come this ___.

      wait   week   woad

We saw a bus come up the ___.

      roach   ray   road

Dig the soil with a fork and put in the ___.

      sheep   seeds   soaps

Shall I poach you an ___?

      arm   egg   oath

Consonant blends

scarf   shelf   sweet   point   ☐

free   moist   snarl   twerp   ☐

smart   green   stay   think   ☐

saw   could   your
rain + storm = rainstorm

I saw your scarf by the green chair. ☐

If you are smart, you will stay away today. ☐

Could you tell your dog not to snarl? ☐

The rainstorm has left the soil moist. ☐

Could you point to the deer you saw? ☐

That twerp thinks the sweets are free. ☐

Could you put your torch back on the top shelf? ☐

128

FLUENCY READING

Timed reading:
☐ Pass: 10 sec.   ☆ Bonus: 8 sec.   ★ Double Bonus: 6 sec.

yon	jerk	week	bib	☐ ☆ ★
herd	hard	den	back	☐ ☆ ★
part	mitt	that	rush	☐ ☆ ★
fad	than	posh	moss	☐ ☆ ★
deck	mash	bid	tick	☐ ☆ ★
bark	luff	with	been	☐ ☆ ★
con	thin	deep	fen	☐ ☆ ★
duck	sheep	Jess	nerd	☐ ☆ ★
sham	gob	Herb	far	☐ ☆ ★

Bart's shack was smart and it was big as well.

Beer with Bart.

Bart said that his shack was smart, for it had a coat of fresh paint. But it was big as well. They went up the stairs, and at the top they saw Bart's maid. She had to mop up the muck, and in a dump this can be a hard job.

"You can put Froid's chair here by this pail of snails", said Bart. "Here is the beer. If you wait, Meg the maid will bring you a glass. Then she will put lunch on the oak board by the stairs."

Mark said, "I am not a big boy, and my mum says I must not drink much beer. Can I have a glass of milk?" Vern said, "I am a big boy, and I drink lots of beer. Put my glass here. Cheers!"

Do you still think that Mark got his lunch?

DECODING POWER PAGE

Do not award ticks for a 'good try'—your pupil will pay for it later!

quick	kerb	rash	fifth	☐
mort	chug	quench	morse	☐
swill	glad	brim	drop	☐
peep	lard	shed	geese	☐
loft	junk	kelp	ink	☐
shack	perch	Seth	pick	☐
brass	grim	spot	swam	☐
pair	shore	deer	oar	☐
tar	baize	tee	noise	☐
sung	jail	wimp	moist	☐

should would could your

Mum said I should put on my ___.

    chop   coat   coach

Wait for your gran in the car ___.

    park   pair   pick

Would you give the horse some ___?

    oaks   oaths   oats

We could go and help put up the ___.

    tamp   tank   tent

Can you give me that pair of your ___?

    soil   sort   socks

My goat lives in that ___.

    shed   sheep   shop

FLUENCY READING

Timed reading:
☐ Pass: 10 sec.   ☆ Bonus: 8 sec.   ★ Double Bonus: 6 sec.

buff	buck	fee	nag	☐ ☆ ★
bath	dish	tod	puck	☐ ☆ ★
peel	mess	sock	shot	☐ ☆ ★
teg	seem	duff	berth	☐ ☆ ★
arm	them	feet	doff	☐ ☆ ★
kick	card	will	dock	☐ ☆ ★
shell	fib	her	carp	☐ ☆ ★
cox	ruck	lash	fid	☐ ☆ ★
then	seed	fern	quack	☐ ☆ ★

Mark has a bath.

Mark said, "Could I have a bath now? My hair is full of moist muck." Bart the damp dog said, "You can go up the stairs and have a bath. Be quick now, or you will miss your lunch." So Mark went up the stairs. The stairs went up and up. They went up so far that Mark could see the stars in the sky.

At last Mark got to the bath. He got in the hot tub with some soap and had a long soak. Then he had to wait for Meg the maid, who had some fresh socks. She said, "Here, let me give you this dress to put on now." "But I am not a lass," Mark said, "I am a boy!" But Mark had to put the dress on, or he would have to go to lunch in just his socks.

Mark got back, but there was no lunch. Groin the gray-green goat was there. The quiff in his hair was stiff with muck. "Have a munch

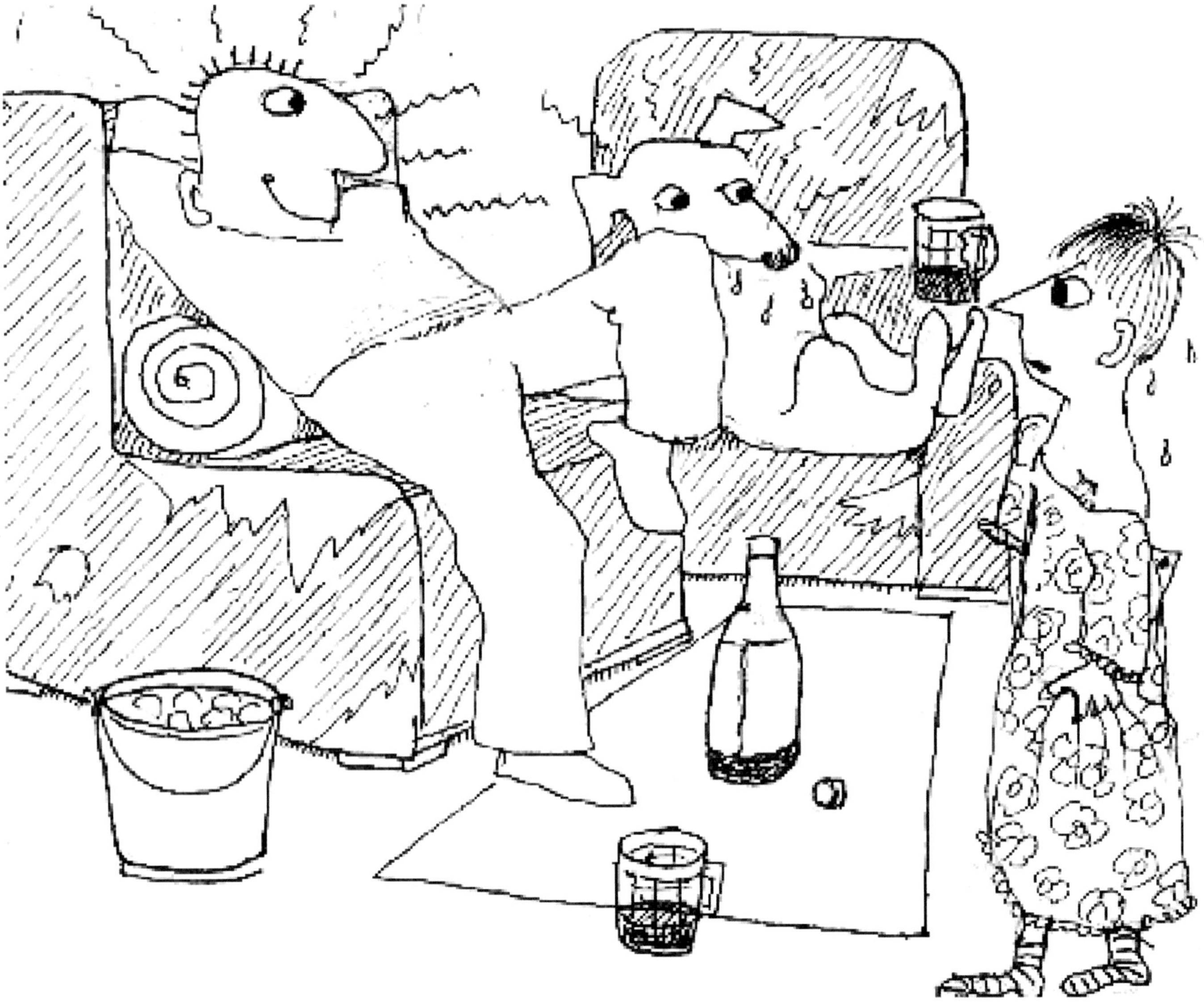

on this board," he said. Vern, Bart and Froid drank the beer, and they could not stand up. "Give a glass of beer to Herb," said Bart, "He cannot come up the stairs, for he is a sharp shark." Mark had to ask, "How did Herb get here? Has he paid ten quid for a bus pass?"

Do you think Mark will ever get his mum some milk and a loaf?

Do you think Mark will ever get some lunch?

You will see when you get your next book!

Mastery Test

Any pupil who does not pass this test must go back to page 124. This is very important—a child who is struggling will not be learning. Contrary to what you would think, children do not mind going back. It's better than getting things wrong.

If the pupil needs to go back, use a different coloured pencil for the tracing exercises and for ticking the boxes.

Timed reading: 'Pass' mark is 15 seconds per line.

spark	score	creep	tray	☐
stern	point	float	quack	☐
brain	chair	coy	stork	☐

Reading accuracy: Pass mark is one mistake.
Do not prompt. You may allow the pupil to self correct, but you cannot say anything except "Try again".

There is still some corn left in the grain store. ☐

Could you put your coat next to her cloak? ☐

Last week, Joan wore her hair in a braid. ☐

We saw where Roy hid his sports bag. ☐

Clair will paint the boards with a green stain. ☐

dancing bears

Well done!

you have completed
Level 3

You are ready to start **dancing bears B**

Other publications from Sound Foundations:

The **dancing bears** decoding series
(All decoding books are consumables, designed for one-on-one teaching)

NEW—**bear necessities**...
... is an "Industrial Strength" version of **Dancing Bears A**. It is suitable especially for beginners and pupils with severe dyslexia.

FAST TRACK...
...is a condensed version of **Dancing Bears A** and **Dancing Bears B**. It is suitable for poor decoders who have a reading age of at least 7 years.

dancing bears B...
...teaches word attack skills for longer words, and more advanced spelling patterns. It follows either **Dancing Bears A** or **Bear Necessities**.

dancing bears C...
...teaches advanced decoding skills. It follows either **Dancing Bears B** or **Fast Track**.

The **apples & pears** spelling series:

Each level of **Apples and Pears** consists of a book of **Teacher's Notes**, plus consumable **Student Workbooks**. They can be used for one-on-one teaching, or they can be used with groups of pupils who are well-matched for ability.

Level **A** and Level **B** are suitable for Infants, as well as older pupils with special needs. Level **C** and Level **D** are suitable for Juniors and above.

These books can all be viewed as PDF read-only files at
www.soundfoundationsbooks.co.uk